D1805973

THEO'S TRAVELS

by

Stanley Sprocket

Theo lived on a green double-decker bus with his mum and dad. His uncle Julien and auntie Coreen also lived in the bus. They travelled all over Europe from the top of Holland to the bottom of Spain.

Theo's dad was from Bath, England. Theo's mum was from Toulouse, France.

Theo was born in Toulouse and celebrated his first birthday in Glastonbury Festival in England. Theo liked the festival.

BONJOUR FRANCE

One day they boarded a huge ship; "The Pride of Napoleon". They were off on a big adventure. Many friends and relatives waved from the quay as the ship slipped its moorings.

Soon the French coastline was out of sight.

Theo loved the indoor swimming pool.

Next morning they arrived in Corsica. There was snow on the mountains, but the beaches were warm and sunny. They took another boat to Sardinia.

CIAO ITALY

Theo's mum and dad were circus performers. They travelled all around Italy busking. Auntie Coreen was in the show too. Uncle Julien would look after Theo. They would go shopping together.

Theo loved the pizza and Italian ice cream. Ice cream shops were everywhere.

For his second birthday he got a bicycle. Uncle Pascal and his enormous dog Cartouche arrived from France. She was bigger than Theo.

HOT IN GREECE

Theo and the others took another boat to Greece. It was very hot. Theo enjoyed swimming in the sea with his water wings. He liked the olives and feta cheese the best.

Sometimes Theo would go into town with the circus and watch the show.

Everyone would squeeze his cheeks. It hurt and he hated it.

TURKEY

In Turkey, they parked up by the Blue Mosque in Istanbul.

He walked through the covered market with his dad. It seemed endless.

On the south coast they lived in tree houses. Theo's house was fortunately close to the ground, but the others lived high up in the trees.

The circus made lots of shows almost every evening in this resort for backpackers. Theo was getting bigger. His uncle Julien built him a new bed with a bookcase for his books and plenty of space for his teddies.

Georgio was his favourite bear and was also head of the bears during all meetings

IRAN

In Iran, Theo's mum and auntie Coreen had to wear chadors. Iran had great fruit juice shops. Theo loved these shops. Pomegranate was his favourite.

He was also a big fan of the special yellow rice mixed with saffron.

Theo's dad had to busk on his own, as women were not allowed to perform.

The Iranian people were very friendly, but the police did not encourage contact with foreigners. Theo however would play with everyone.

PAKISTAN

Pakistan had the brightest trucks Theo had ever seen. The roads were very rough. In the Baluchistan desert most of the circus rode ahead of the bus on their bicycles. It was much less bumpy than being in the bus and certainly faster.

Theo rode in a basket attached to the handlebars with either his dad or his uncle Julien. Theo's dad would get out the cricket bat and ball and play with the locals.

Theo lived on fruit, white rice and chapattis made freshly from a hot earth oven. The curry was too spicy for him. Sometimes it was too hot for his mum and dad too.

INDIA

The first place Theo went to in India was the Golden Temple in Amritsar. It was an amazing temple with people constantly singing and playing music.

The roads were a chaotic mess of people, bicycles, carts, cars, trucks and cows. In India cows are sacred. Nobody eats cows, but their milk is used to make chai, a hot sweet tea like drink. The circus spent the season in Goa and took part in Carnival.

Theo played cricket on the beach, swam in the sea and ate lots of papaya and coconuts. Theo was still learning to swim. Pascal, Cartouche and auntie Coreen left for Peru.

NEPAL

In Nepal, Theo went trekking in the Himalayas. Sarah and Steve, who had flown out from England played music with his mum and dad in the show. Sometimes Theo would take part too.

In Kathmandu, Theo started going to school. He liked school and invited lots of his friends for his third birthday party.

Grandma Audrey and Grandpa Geoffrey arrived too with lots of presents.

BANGLADESH

Bangladesh was a very crowded country. There would always be lots of people around the bus. It was also a very flat country. Rickshaws filled the streets and were much more popular than cars.

Many of the people's homes had been flooded, forcing them to live by the roadside. They all smiled and waved when the bus went by. Theo waved back.

BURMA

The circus tried to drive to Burma. The map they had showed a road, but as they drove towards the border, the road got smaller and smaller.

At the customs border they found a river, but no bridge. They had to turn back.

Instead they sent the bus from Chittagong to Singapore on a container ship. The bus was winched on board by a huge crane. It looked so small on the huge ship. Theo's bears looked very scared.

Theo and the circus flew to Singapore to meet it. It was Theo's first ride in an airplane. It was very exciting.

SINGAPORE

Singapore was a very modern country. The buildings were the tallest Theo had ever seen.

They watched the ship arrive and the unloading of the bus. Theo checked on all his bears. In Singapore, everyone had mobile telephones so Theo got one too; a toy one. Theo visited the zoo. He'd seen lots of elephants in India, but this was the first time he'd rode on one.

MALAYSIA

In Desaru, they parked the bus by the beach and went swimming. The bus was invaded by a group of monkeys who opened everything in the kitchen; cereals, jams and yoghurt making a terrible mess. Theo's passport was covered in marmalade. Malaysia had lots of forests, but it was very, very hot.

They headed off to the Cameron Highlands where it was much cooler. Theo and his dad played a round of golf; both of them had a caddie. The engine of the bus broke. It had to be rebuilt which took many months.

THAILAND

They sped north towards Thailand. The Circus took a boat to Koh Samui where they stayed for a couple of months whilst his parents performed on the island. They lived in a beach house and Theo went to another school.

Theo went to a full moon party on Ko Pha Ngang. Theo called the moon Angelo. He would shout "hello Angelo" at the top of his voice, but only when the stars came out and he was sure Angelo was awake.

 When he woke up the party was still going on. He liked dancing and drinking coconut milk straight out of coconuts.

INDONESIA

Rocking Chance joined them. He was a bear that also acted as a backpack. He guided Theo's mum, dad and uncle Julien through the jungles and down rivers. Theo loved the sweet rice and all the strange new fruits.

The bus was on its way to Australia. Theo needed a visa.In Bali, the Australian embassy gave him one.

AUSTRALIA

They landed by plane in Perth, Western Australia. A few days later the bus arrived in Fremantle.

They travelled north to Darwin. Sometimes kangaroos would bounce into the road in front of the bus then bounce off into the distance. In Kakadu National Park, Theo saw lots of crocodiles. He was very scared of them, but they did not attack the boat he was in.

He travelled south to see Ayers Rock. Many travellers joined the circus as they travelled across this immense country. They travelled to Melbourne and Sydney before reaching Queensland. It was very hot.

Theo and the circus were asked to leave Australia for not having work permits for the show.

NEW ZEALAND

New Zealand was a much more friendly country. Theo was given a student visa and the others were given work visas.

He went to his first big school in Golden Bay in the South Island. He was now five years old. He liked school and all his classmates. He also started performing with his mum and dad. He did a diabolo act.

New Zealand was where Theo learnt to ride a bicycle and how to ski.

 It was a very green country with huge mountains.

Over a year had passed and it was time to move on to South America. His uncle Julien decided to stay in New Zealand.

HOLA CHILE

In Chile there were circus performers everywhere, even performing at the traffic lights.

Theo had to go to school and learn Spanish. It was very difficult, but he learnt it so he could play with the other children. The circus teamed up with Pato-Giro, Mauricio and Felipe, all from Chile. They became his friends. He called them his brothers.

Theo liked the avocados. He also liked bebidas and dulces (fizzy drinks and sweets).

Theo celebrated his seventh birthday party in Copiapo, a large mining town.

PERU

In Peru, Theo had his BMX bike stolen. He was very sad. He had been given it in New Zealand.

They stopped in Lima. The circus made lots of shows. Theo went to another school. The circus came and did their show there.

At the beach they ate ceviche, a seafood dish. Dad ate fruit. He didn't like fish. Theo played football in the street. He liked football, but some of the other boys were very good.

ECUADOR

In Ecuador, they found a town called Baños with naturally hot water. It was too hot for Theo.

Bananas were very cheap. Theo tried to lift a bunch onto the bus. It was too heavy.

In Quito, Theo started at the French school, where everybody spoke French. His French was not very good, but he understood it as he had travelled with his uncle Julien for many years.

COLUMBIA.

Columbia was a very beautiful country with friendly people. Everyone loved the shows. There were lots of checkpoints. Sometimes Theo would show the police his bedroom where his bears were. He now had over 20 teddy bears.

In Cali, Theo went to another French school. They parked the bus in the woods next to a circus school with a big top.

For Theo's eighth birthday they parked the bus at a go-kart course. Theo went round and around the circuit only stopping for fruits, cakes and drinks.

VENEZUELA

Dad was pleased with the price of fuel. He said it was 100 times more expensive in England. Theo would help him fill up. Sometimes they'd stop over a pit to service and grease the bus.

Theo found a small abandoned dog on the beach and decided to adopt him. He called him Julio. Some of the other bears got jealous. Dragon decided to fight Julio, but ended up losing and had to have his foot stitched up by mum.

They found a roll-on roll-off ship and sent the bus to North America. Disneyland and Disney World were not far away thought Theo.

PANAMA

Theo stayed at The Summit', a park and zoo on the edge of Panama City. He found a very sad and lonely monkey trapped in a cage.

Together with the head zoo keeper, who knew Cobi the monkey would soon die of loneliness, they smuggled him out of the zoo.

They found him a place by the beach where there were other monkeys for him to play with. "He'll be safe and happy here" said Theo.

In Panama, Theo met up with Jo, his new French teacher. Jo was from France and helped Theo learn his school through a correspondence course.

COSTA RICA

Costa Rica had some of the best beaches Theo had ever seen. He learnt how to surf in Porto Viejo on the Atlantic coast. Mum and dad loved the coffee, but Theo was always happy with coco-rice and beans.

Heading north, one of the bridges had broken. They had to drive the bus through the river.

Theo's dog was run over and killed by a fast moving car. Theo was very sad. "If I ever have another dog, I'll teach him to watch out" said Theo.

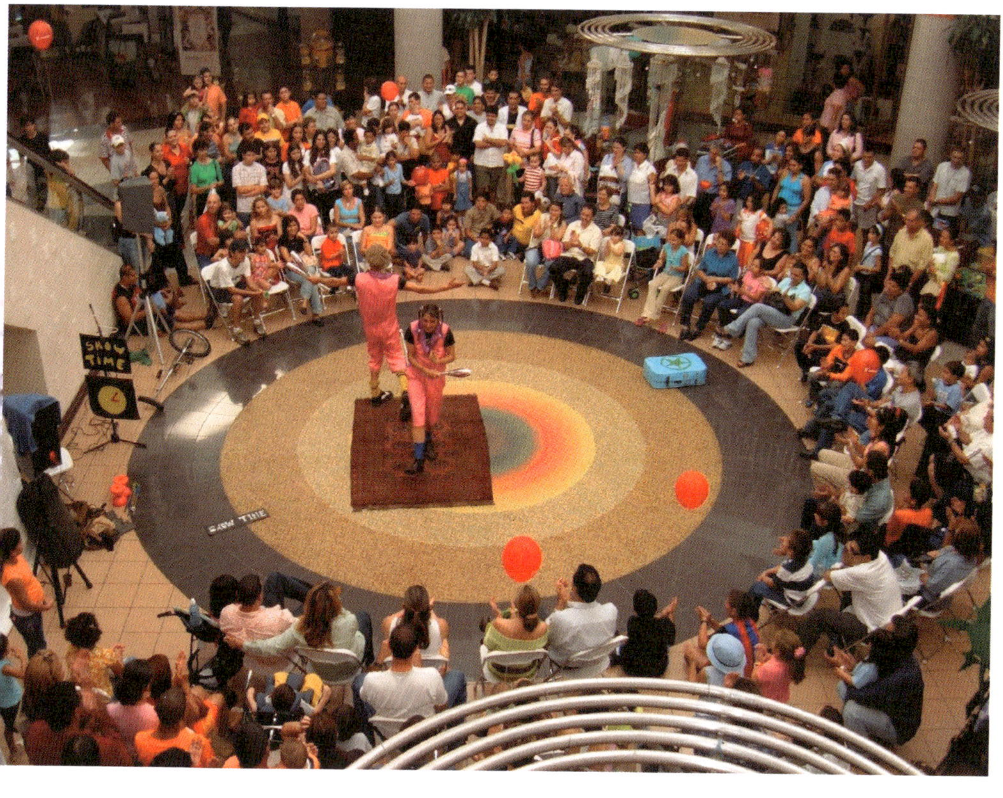

NICARAGUA

It was full into the rainy season by the time they entered Nicaragua. The roads were rough and muddy and many of the houses were flooded.

Theo made friends with the shoeshine boys, who polished shoes in the plaza. He started to earn money too by selling his drawings. He liked drawing.

Theo's Spanish was much better now compared to his humble beginnings in Chile years earlier. There were always new words to learn and pronounce.

HONDURAS

The circus visited some Maya temples surrounded by thick jungle. In one town, Theo joined the other children in a game of jumping on and off the back of motorised rickshaws.

Unfortunately the rickshaw was going too fast to get off and he found himself lost at the bus station. Luckily somebody helped him find the bus again. He learned a big lesson.

EL SALVADOR

The capital city San Salvador was very chaotic, but fun. As they passed the market Theo could buy things through the window without leaving the bus.

Theo loved eating Pupasas, a cheesy vegetable bread snack that was sold everywhere.

Theo's dad needed to change some of his tyres.

The circus got a booking to do their show in a town called Suchitoto. They were invited to go canoeing on a lake.

GUATEMALA

In Guatemala the circus parked up next to Lake Atitlan. His mum and dad made circus shows at 'The Circus Bar' in Panajachel. Theo would cycle his bike to the market in town with his dad and teacher Jo to buy fruit and vegetables. Sometimes they would cross the lake by boat to do shows.

They stopped in Antigua. This was a city surrounded by volcanos.

In Guatemala City, they met up with Panchoriso, another street performer and together they celebrated his dad's birthday with a show for the locals.

MEXICO

Mexico was a vast country. They travelled through Chiapas to Tulum on the Yucatán coast. The beaches were beautiful and Theo would go snorkelling with his friends.

Sometimes they would pick up shells from the beach and sell them to tourists. Theo celebrated his 10th birthday in Chalula, just south of Mexico City.

In Zacatecas, where the circus was booked to perform in a festival, the engine broke down. Luckily they were able to fix it.

Theo would sometimes perform shows with his dad and spend his share of the hat in video gaming shops called 'maquinitas'.

CUBA

Theo and the circus flew to Cuba with their Mexican tricycle. They performed with a local circus group on the streets of La Habana.

It was great fun parading through the streets with the Samba band and stilt walkers. Theo liked music. Everyone joined in dancing, even the street cleaner.

Mum and dad tried the Cuban cigars and rum. Theo loved riding around in the 1950's American cars. They had huge bench seats and ornate dashboards.

The circus flew back to Mexico to pick up their bus and began driving towards the States.

U.S.A.

In the USA, the bus was too slow to travel on the interstate highways, so Theo got to see the 'real' America, travelling the back roads. The circus made shows on both the East and West Coast's, which meant Theo could visit both Disneyland and Disney World. He preferred Disneyland in Los Angeles, as it was friendlier and he got to ride in Walt Disney's car. His favourite ride was 'Space Mountain'.

In Texas, he began helping the waitresses in 'The Starlight Theatre' where his mum and dad were performing their show. He helped serve the water to the customers and made great money in tips. The bus engine began breaking again. Luckily mum could fix it. Dad was a useless mechanic.

CANADA

The first province the circus visited was Quebec, where they speak French. In Ontario, Canada, Theo visited Niagara Falls with his cousins, Flora and Ed, who had come to visit him once again.

Canada had lots of wild empty spaces, thousands of lakes and seemingly endless highways. Theo had to study on the road with his mum, as Jo had flown back to France. The bus was also his school.

They crossed Canada from East to West, passing over the snowy mountains and into British Colombia.

It was time to head back to Europe. In New York, they put the bus on another huge ship bound for Southampton, England.

EUROPE

It was the end of a big adventure and the beginning of another.

The circus moved back to Italy. Theo found another abandoned street dog in Sicily and named her Shara.

They still perform with the bus and Theo's a big boy now, but still travels with his mum and dad.

So if you see a large green double-decker bus, toot and wave.

Happy travels

The End

SHARA THE DOG

55832888R00040

Made in the USA
Charleston, SC
06 May 2016